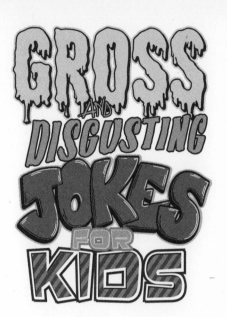

GROSS AND DISGUSTING JOKES FOR KIDS

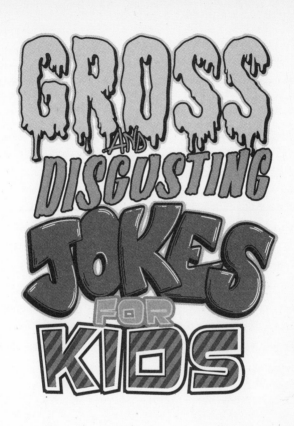

GROSS AND DISGUSTING JOKES FOR KIDS

by James Allan Einstein
with illustrations by Roger Garcia Einstein

BLUE
BIKE
BOOKS

The Publisher: Blue Bike Books
Website: www.bluebikebooks.com

Library and Archives Canada Cataloguing in Publication

Einstein, James Allan, 1977–, author
        Gross & disgusting jokes for kids / James Allan Einstein.

ISBN 978-1-926700-45-8 (pbk.)

        1. Canadian wit and humor (English). 2. Wit and humor, Juvenile. I. Title. II. Title: Gross and disgusting jokes for kids.

PN6178.C3E33 2014   jC818'.602   C2013-906422-2

Project Director: "Mama" Nicholle Carrière Einstein
Project Editor: "Sista" Kathy van Denderen Einstein
Cover Images: Front cover - texture in "Gross" lettering © vladajv / Photos.com; yellow ink splats behind the "Gross" lettering © Carl Eriksson / Photos.com; little purple monster illustration © Pedro Guillermo Angeles-Flores / Photos.com; green slime monster illustration © Pedro Guillermo Angeles-Flores / Photos.com; back cover - little purple monster illustration © Pedro Guillermo Angeles-Flores / Photos.com; zit popping illustration © Anthony Oshlick / Photos.com; snot nose and glasses illustration Roger Garcia Einstein
Cover Design: Gerry Dotto Einstein
Illustrations: Roger Garcia Einstein, Photos.com
Layout: "Sista" Alesha Braitenbach-Cartledge Einstein

Produced with the assistance of the
Government of Alberta, Alberta Media Fund.

Alberta Government

We acknowledge the financial support of the Government of Canada through the Canada Book Fund (CBF) for our publishing activities.

 Canadian   Patrimoine
Heritage   canadien

PC: 24

See What's Yucky Inside

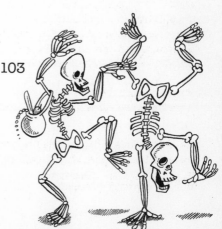

Introduction

Welcome

to the wonderful world of gross and disgusting jokes—
the kids-only edition. Why do most people never
remember a joke? Because most of the jokes aren't
memorable enough, that's why! As you make your
way through this book, I guarantee that you will come
across more than one joke (or seven) that will
annoyingly and disgustingly stick inside your head.
"Why did the chicken cross the road?" is boring and
common, but "How do you get a Kleenex to dance?"
(Answer: By putting a little boogie in it!) is a joke
you'll want to share with as many people as possible.

However, I do offer a word of warning. If you think
that booger joke is gross, then this book is definitely
not for you. If you find boogies yucky, then these jokes
will make you run to the bathroom or search for an
airplane barf bag. Why, just the first chapter alone
will make you pee your pants as you read through
jokes about breaking wind and other wonderful

functions of the human body. If you can make it through this chapter, then the rest of the book is right up your alley because the jokes get even more gross and disgusting.

So sit back, read a few jokes and please try not to soil yourself as you laugh out loud at some of these really unpleasant but hilarious jokes—because if you do, you just might make it into the second edition of the book.

And remember, kids, whoopee cushions will always be funny!

Chapter ONE

Things that ooze, fart or Stink

Hey, kids, think of farts as a wish your butt makes.

Ladies, first

Two teenage couples are at a dinner party, when one guy farts.

The other young man says, "How dare you fart in front of my girlfriend!"

The first guy says, "Oh, I'm sorry. I didn't realize it was her turn."

Do You Believe in Magic?

A very good magician has hypnotized an entire audience. He has them under his complete control, and

Question:
Why do farts smell?

Answer:
So deaf people can enjoy them, too.

they are willing to do whatever he tells them to do.

Unfortunately, at the vital moment, he trips over the microphone cord, lands on his bum and says, "Crap!"

Question:
Why did Spock look in the toilet?

Answer:
To see the captain's log.

Cover Music

A guy is sitting at a concert and needs to fart. The music is so loud that he just decides to go for it and times his farts to the beat of the music. After he is finished, he looks up to see the people around him staring at him. He suddenly realizes that he is listening to his iPod.

Busy!

Little Red Riding Hood is walking around in the forest with her basket and in the distance she sees the Big Bad Wolf. Little Red Riding Hood goes up to the wolf and says, "Big Bad Wolf, why do you have such little eyes?"

The wolf replies, "Oh, go away, you! I'm taking a poop!"

To Battle We Go!

A ship captain is sailing on the sea during a battle. His servant goes up to him and asks him what to do. The captain says, "Bring me my red shirt."

So the servant does as the captain orders.

The servant then asks the captain, "Why did you want me to bring you a red shirt?"

The captain replies, "Well, if I get shot, the enemy won't see the blood."

The next day, the servant goes up to the captain and says, "Captain, there are 50 ships on the horizon! What should I do?"

The captain says, "Bring me my brown pants."

Silent and Deadly

A man is visiting his doctor.

The doctor says, "What seems to be the problem today, Mr. Smith?"

The man says, "Well, doc, I've got the farts...I mean, I fart all the time."

The doctor nods and says, "Hmm. That's interesting."

Question:
Why didn't the skeleton cross the road?

Answer:
It had no guts.

"The funny thing is that my farts don't stink at all!" says the man. "And no one can hear them. I fart all the time. For example, we've been talking for about five minutes or so, and I've farted five times already! You didn't hear them, and you didn't smell them, did you?"

"Hmm," says the doctor. He then gives the man some pills to take.

The man is very happy. "Doc, will these pills really clear up my farts?"

"No," says the doctor. "The pills will clear your sinuses. You need to come back to see me next week for a hearing test."

Football Farts

A husband and his wife are in bed watching football. After a few minutes, the husband lets rip a big fart. His wife rolls over and growls, "What was that?"

The husband says, "Touchdown! I'm ahead, seven to nothing!"

A few seconds later, the wife lets rip a big fart.

The husband says, "Wow, what was that?"

She replies, "Touchdown, tie score."

The man lays there for about 10 minutes trying to work up a bigger fart. He tries so hard he accidentally poops in the bed.

The wife asks, "Now what in the world was that?"

Her husband replies, "It's halftime, now we switch sides."

Question:
Why did the blonde throw breadcrumbs in the toilet every morning?

Answer:
To feed the toilet duck.

Farts in Rhyme

He who declared it, blared it.
He who observed it, served it.
He who detected it, ejected it.
He who said the rhyme did the crime.
Whoever spoke last, set off the blast.
Whoever smelt it, dealt it.

Whoever denied it, supplied it.

The next person who speaks is the person who reeks.

The smeller's the feller.

The one who said the verse just made the atmosphere worse.

Whoever's poking fun is the smoking gun.

He who accuses, blew the fuses.

He who refuted it, tooted it.

He who pointed the finger, pulled the finger.

He who deduced it, produced it.

He who sniffed it, biffed it.

Whoever makes the joke makes the bum smoke.

He who rapped it, cracked it.

Whoever rebuts it, cuts it.

Whoever spoke it, broke it.

Whoever asked, gassed.

Whoever started, farted.

Whoever explained it, ordained it.

Whoever described it, applied it.

Whoever thunk it, stunk it.

Whoever resented it, presented it.

Whoever accused it, diffused it.

Whoever spoke the words is baking the turds.

Wizard Wishes

Three men win a contest. Their prize is a wish from a wizard. All three men wish for a toilet.

The first man wants a wooden toilet. So the wizard grants his wish.

The second man wants a metal toilet. He also gets his wish.

The third man wants a talking toilet. He gets his wish.

The next day, the three men all want to return their toilets.

The first man says to the wizard, "My toilet is rotted through." So the wizard takes back his toilet.

Question:
What happened to the blind skunk?

Answer:
He fell in love with a fart.

The second one says, "My toilet is all rusted." So the wizard takes his toilet back, too.

The third man says, "Every time I try to sit on the toilet to use it, it starts to sing 'I see your hinny, all white and shiny, if you don't hide it, I'm gonna bite it.'"

Fart Poetry

A fart can be quiet,
A fart can be loud,
Some leave a powerful,
Poisonous cloud.

A fart can be short,
Or a fart can be long,
Some farts have been known,
To sound just like a song.

Some farts do not smell,
While others are vile,
A fart may pass quickly,
Or linger awhile.

A fart can create
A most-curious medley,
A fart can be harmless,
Or silent, but deadly.

A fart can occur
In a number of places,
And leave everyone
With strange looks on their faces.

From wide-open prairies,
To small elevators,
A fart will find all of us
Sooner or later.

So be not afraid
Of the invisible gas,
For always remember,
That farts, too, shall pass.

When You Should Never Fart

1. Inside a crowded elevator.
2. Inside a school library.
3. On a crowded bus.
4. While giving a speech.
5. In church.
6. While on a first date.
7. In a packed classroom.
8. At the dinner table.
9. At a movie theater.
10. In the ticket line while buying popcorn.
11. In a walk-in freezer—it'll stay a while.
12. On an airplane.

In the Bathtub

What's gross?
Farting in the bathtub.

What's grosser than that? Catching the bubbles with your teeth.

Honda!

A young man goes to the doctor and says, "You have to help me. Every time I fart, it sounds like 'Honda.'"

The doctor says, "You say, 'Honda' when you fart?"

"No," the man says. "My *farts* do."

The doctor says, "Okay, open your mouth," and he looks inside.

After two minutes, the doctor says, "I'm sorry, I can't help you. You need to see a dentist."

The young man says, "Why a dentist?"

The doctor says, "Because you have an abscessed tooth."

"What does that have to do with my problem?"

The doctor says, "Well, didn't you know? Abscess makes the farts go Honda!"

Question:
What do you get when you mix beans and onions?

Answer:
Tear gas.

I Think I'm Going to be Sick

What's grosser than gross?
When you throw your underwear and it sticks to the wall.

What's grosser than that?
Watching it crawl down.

What's grosser than that?
Watching it crawl back up again.

What's grosser than that?
Watching it fly back at you.

Types of farts

Arrogant Fart: When you think your farts don't stink.

Assault Fart: A sudden attack that shoots flames out of your bum.

Brain Fart: You need to fart, but nothing comes out.

Ghost Fart: You can't hear it, you can't see it and you can't smell it.

Jail Fart: It's been doing time inside you for quite a while and finally makes its great escape.

Home-alone Fart: When you're home alone and a great one is wasted on no one.

Not-me Fart: When you fart in a crowded elevator, turn around to the person behind you and give a disgusted look and whisper "Pig!"

Old Fart: You know how old it is by how bad it smells.

Shoe Fart: When you bend over to tie your shoelaces and one escapes.

Tank Fart: When you refer to your farts as "gas."

Tire Fart: You can't control the blow out.

UFO Fart: When someone farts in a crowded room, it's called an "Unidentified Foul Odor."

Question:
Did ya hear that diarrhea is hereditary?

Answer:
Yeah, it runs in the jeans.

other Names for Puking

Airing the diced carrots

Barfing

Being the mother bird

Big spit

Bowing down at the porcelain god

Bracking

Bringing it up for a vote

Bushing breakfast

Casting your bread upon the waters

Chewing backwards

Chooming

Chucking

Cleaning house

Decorating the pavement

Divulging dinner

Draining the main

Dribbling phlegm

Driving the porcelain bus

Ejecting

Feedback

Feeding your young

Fertilizing the sidewalk

Filling the bilge

Gacking

Gagging

Gurping

Gut painting

Hacking

Harfing

Having a rerun of your lunch

Heaving (your guts out)

Honking

Horking

Hurling

Involuntary personal protein spill

Jump shot

Lateral cookie toss

Launching lunch

Launching the shuttle

Liquid scream

Losing some chopped carrots

Losing weight

Losing your lunch

Making pizza

Negative chug

Painting the town green

Polishing your shoes

Power barf, boot

Projectiling

Protein spill

Psychedelic spit

Purging the system

Ralphing

Redecorating

Retching

Reverse diarrhea

Revisiting dinner

Riding the regurgitation

Round-trip lunch ticket, meal ticket

Screaming cookies

Shouting at your shoes

Spewing

Spilling the groceries

Talking to the whales

Tasting dinner

Throwing dinner

Tossing your cookies

Upchucking

Voiding

Vomiting

Waxing the floor

Whistling beef

Wolfing

Yakking

Yelling at the ground

What's gross?

When you open the fridge and the rump roast farts in your face.

And You Thought Picking Your Nose Was Just Picking Your Nose

Autopick: The kind of picking you do when no one is looking. This can also mean "automatic pick"—the picking you do when you're not even thinking about it—maybe while at school talking to a buddy during class.

Deep Salvage Pick: This is like a deep-sea exploration to find the *Titanic* ship, when you poke deep into your nose.

Depression Pick: When you're sad and bored, and the only way to fill the time is to pick so hard and fast that you feel much better after.

Extra Pick: When you have been digging for nuggets for hours and suddenly you hit the jackpot. It's like you've won the lottery!

Fake Nose Scratch: When you pretend you have an itchy nose, but you're really checking for stray boogers.

Hidden Kiddie Pick: When around other people, you wrap your index finger in a tissue, then thrust it in deep and hold back the smile.

Question:
What's the definition of "suffocation"?

Answer:
Egg farts in a spacesuit.

Kiddie Pick: When you're by yourself and you twist your index finger into your nose with joy and freedom. And the best part is, there's no time limit!

Making a Meal Out of It: You pick your nose so furiously and for so long that you probably deserve to have dessert.

Pick a Lot: This is when you do an abnormal amount of picking.

Pick and Flick: You use snot as a weapon against your sister and others around you.

Pick and Save: When you have to pick your nose quickly—at the exact moment when the person next to you looks away—and then you pocket the snot so they don't catch on to what you did.

Pick and Stick: You wanted it to be a "Pick and Flick," but it stubbornly clings to your fingertip.

Pipe Cleaner Pick: The kind where you remove a piece of snot so big, it improves your breathing by 90 percent.

Pick Your Brains: This is done in private, where your finger goes in so far that it almost tickles your brain.

Surprise Pickings: When a sneeze or laugh makes snot come hurling out of your nose, and you have to very carefully clean it off your shirt.

Utensil Pick: When your fingers, and even your thumb, just aren't enough to get the job done so you have to use something else.

Who Picks?

Now that you know what kind of picking is out there, here is a list of how many people pick their noses (and the gross things they do when they find something). Some scientists somewhere thought it would be a good idea to look into people's nose-picking habits. These are the results.

- 8 percent of the people said that they have never picked their nose. (In other words, they are liars, or they can't remember doing it as a kid.)
- 91 percent stated that they had picked their nose in the past and still do. But only 49 percent of the people actually thought that nose-picking was common in adults.

- 9 percent rate their pickin' as "more than average."
- 25 percent pick their noses daily, 22 percent do it 2–5 times each day and three people admitted to doing it at least hourly. (Wow, how bored are they?)
- 55 percent spend 1–5 minutes each day cleaning their noses, 23 percent spend 5–15 minutes and 0.8 percent (two people) spend 15–30 minutes picking their noses. One man said he picked his nose for more than two hours every day. (I'm no doctor, but I think this guy has a big problem or a really, really big nose!)
- 18 percent of the people said they had nosebleeds, and 0.8 percent said that they had injured their nose from all that picking.
- 65 percent use their index finger, 20 percent use their pinky and 16 percent use their thumb (they must have big nostrils) as their "instrument" of choice.
- Most people (90 percent) got rid of the goop in a tissue or a handkerchief, 28 percent used the floor and 7 percent stuck it onto a piece of furniture. (Don't reach under your desk!)
- 8 percent said they ate what they found. In case you are thinking of trying this, the people said that the "pickings" are quite tasty (salty).

Question:
How does Edward Scissor Hands wipe his bum?

Answer:
Very, very carefully!

Chapter Two

Adults Are Gross and Weird

If four out of five people suffer from diarrhea, does that mean that one enjoys it?

Smelly Feet and Smelly Breath

A young couple is on their honeymoon. The husband is sitting in the bathroom on the edge of the bathtub and says to himself, "How can I tell my wife that I've got really smelly feet and that my socks absolutely stink? I was able to keep it from her while we were dating, but she's going to find out sooner or later that my feet stink. How do I tell her?"

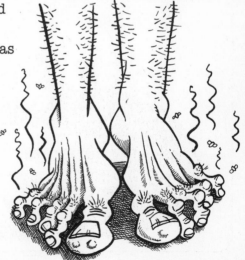

Meanwhile, the wife is sitting on the bed

saying to herself, "How do I tell my husband that I've got really bad breath? I've been very lucky to keep it from him while we were dating, but as soon as we live together, he'll find out. How do I tell him gently?"

The husband finally gets up his courage to tell his wife and walks into the bedroom. He climbs into bed, puts his arm around her neck, moves his face very close to hers and says, "Darling, I've a confession to make."

And she says, "So have I, love."

He replies, "Don't tell me, you've eaten my socks!"

I See

Teacher: "Oh dear! I've lost another pupil."

Principal: "How did that happen?"

Teacher: "My glass eye flew out the window while I was driving."

Question:
What did the turd say to the butt?

Answer:
"I don't ever want to go through that again!"

What's Up, Doc?

A guy goes to see his doctor because he is sick. After examining the man, the doctor says, "Well, I'm afraid you have only six weeks to live."

The guy says, "Oh, that's awful! What should I do, doctor?"

The doctor tells him, "You should take a mud bath once a day for the next six weeks."

The guy asks, "Why? Is that supposed to help?"

The doctor says, "No, but it'll get you used to being in the ground."

Arghhhh!

A pirate walks into a coffee bar with a steering wheel on the front of his pants.

The clerk asks, "What's with the wheel, mister?"

The pirate says, "Arrrr! It drives me nuts!"

Doctor's Advice

Before going on an ocean cruise, a man visits his doctor and tells him that he's worried about getting seasick.

The doctor says, "Eat two pounds of stewed tomatoes before the ships leaves the dock."

The guy replies, "Will that keep me from getting sick?"

The doctor says, "No, but it'll look really pretty in the water!"

A Close Shave

A man goes into a barbershop to get a shave. While the barber is foaming his face, the man says he has a problem getting a close shave around his cheeks.

"I have just the thing," says the barber, who removes a small wooden ball from a drawer. "Just place this ball between your cheek and gum."

The man places the ball in his mouth, and the barber gives him the closest shave he has ever had. After a few strokes, the man asks in garbled speech, "And what if I swallow the ball?"

Question:
What did the judge say when the skunk walked into the courtroom?

Answer:
Odor in the court!

"No problem," says the barber. "Just bring it back tomorrow like everyone else does."

What's Gross?

Bill: "Know what's gross?"

John: "No, what?"

Bill: "Finding a hair in your food. Know what's grosser than gross?"

John: "What?"

Bill: "Finding out that it's your grandma's nose hair!"

Wishes

Two men are walking down the street and see a dog on the lawn, licking himself.

One man says to the other, "Wow, I sure wish I could do that."

The second man says, "Don't you think you oughta pet him first?"

Question:
What has four wheels and flies?

Answer:
A garbage truck.

A Big Stomach

Question:
What did the mother say to the father when their baby boy fell down the stairs?

Answer:
"Oh, look, honey! Our little boy is taking his first 23 steps!"

A wife sees her husband weigh himself on the scale, and he is trying to pull in his stomach. The wife thinks he is trying to reduce his weight on the scale by holding in his stomach. She says to him, "You know, I don't think that will help you."

The husband says, "Of course it helps! It's the only way I can see the number on the scale."

Smells Like?

A guy is driving down the road and picks up a young hitchhiker.

"Hop in!" the driver says. One mile down the road, the driver smells something really bad and asks the guy, "Hey, did you crap your pants?"

The hitchhiker says, "No!"

Two miles down the road, the smell gets worse, and the driver says, "Are you sure you didn't crap your pants?"

The hitchhiker says, "Yes, I'm sure. I didn't."

Three miles down the road, the driver can't stand the smell and stops the car. He yells, "Get out!"

The hitchhiker and the driver get out of the car.

The driver says, "I don't believe you. Pull your pants down."

So the hiker pulls his pants down, and there's poop everywhere. All down his legs.

"I thought you said you didn't poop your pants!" screams the driver.

"Oh, I thought you meant today."

Growing Old Is Great?

Two old men from a retirement home are sitting on a bench under a tree when one turns to the other and says, "John, I'm 83 years old now, and I have a lot of aches and pains. I know you're about my age. How do you feel?"

John says, "I feel just like a newborn baby."

"Really!? Like a newborn baby!?"

"Yep. No hair, no teeth, and I think I just pooped my pants!"

Question:
How do you get a man to stop biting his nails?

Answer:
Make him wear shoes.

Ewwww, Grandpa!

Two old men are eating breakfast in a restaurant one morning.

Ed notices something funny about Joe's ear. He says, "Joe, did you know you have a suppository in your left ear?"

"I do? A suppository, you say?"

Joe pulls it out of his ear and stares at it for a few seconds. Then he says, "Ed, I'm glad you saw this thing. Now I think I know where my hearing aid is."

Good ole Grandpa

One young boy says to his friend, "When I die, I want to go peacefully like my grandfather did, in his sleep—not screaming, like the passengers in his car."

Before Pimple Cream

A long, long time ago, there once was a family of pimple suckers. This family's job was sucking pimples for anyone who needed their service.

One day, the king's daughter gets a pimple, so the king decides to hire the family of pimple suckers to help his daughter. The king calls the family "the royal pimple suckers," so only royalty can use them. The king's daughter is ugly, and the only time she ever gets someone's lips on her is when she gets one of her pimples sucked. She is always happy when she gets a pimple.

One day she gets a huge pimple on her butt, so she calls in one of the royal pimple suckers. He arrives in her room, and she raises her skirt and reveals her pimple. The royal pimple sucker gathers up his courage and starts sucking on the pimple. The princess is very happy and excited, so much so that she let's out a little fart. Right after she farts, the royal pimple sucker jumps back with surprise and says, "Ugh! What are you trying to do...kill me?"

Bob Loves Beans

A teenager named Bob absolutely loves baked beans, but they always make him fart. After he meets the girl of his dreams, he decides to make a big sacrifice and gives up eating beans.

On his birthday a few weeks later, his car breaks down on the way to visiting his girlfriend, Sarah, so he calls her and says he will have to walk to her house.

He then walks past an IHOP and smells the wonderful aroma of baked beans. Since he is still a couple of miles from Sarah's home, he thinks he can still eat the beans and can let out the farts before he gets there. So he has three extra-large helpings of beans, and he farts all the way to his girlfriend's house.

When he gets there, Sarah meets him at the door and is very excited. She says, "Sweetie, I have the most wonderful surprise for you for dinner tonight!"

She blindfolds him and leads him to his chair at the head of the table, making him promise not to peek. Bob is beginning to feel another fart coming on. Just as Sarah is about to remove the blindfold, her cellphone rings and she goes to the living room to answer it.

While she is gone, Bob decides to let out a fart. He leans over and lets one go. The fart is not only loud, but it also smells as ripe as a rotten egg. Bob feels for a napkin on the table and begins to fan the air around him. He is just starting to feel better, when another urge comes on. This one sounds like a truck engine revving and smells even worse. He tries flapping his arms, to clear the air. But another huge fart sneaks out, and the windows rattle, the dishes on the table shake and the flowers on the table die.

When Bob hears Sarah walking back into the room, he quickly puts his napkin on his lap and folds his

Question:
What did one tonsil say to the other tonsil?

Answer:
Get dressed up—the doctor is taking us out.

hands on top of it. He looks totally innocent when she walks in.

After apologizing for taking so long, Sarah asks him if he has peeked at the dinner. Bob tells her that he hasn't, so she removes the blindfold and yells, "Surprise!"

To his shock and horror, there are six dinner guests seated around the table for his surprise birthday party!

Farmer's Son

A young man has been driving for hours on the highway, and he needs to go pee. He stops his truck outside a farmhouse and asks the farmer if he can use his toilet.

"Sure you can, but I gotta warn you, it's a bit of a mess," replies the farmer. "You see, my son takes salts."

The guy thinks that is a strange answer as he walks to the bathroom at the back of the house. When he enters the bathroom, he sees poop all over the ceiling, floors, wall and toilet. He uses it anyway and makes his

Question:
What do you call a dog with no legs?

Answer:
Nothing. It won't come to you when you call it anyway.

ADULTS ARE GROSS AND WEIRD

escape outside as quickly as possible, but he stops to thank the farmer.

"By the way," asks the young guy, "what kind of salts does your son take?"

"Er, somersaults!" replies the farmer.

Question:
Did you hear about the new principal who is keeping all the boys on their toes?

Answer:
He raised all the urinals in the washroom six inches.

Old People's Problem

An old man goes to his doctor and says, "I have this toilet problem, doc."

"Well," replies the doctor, "how's your peeing?"

"Well, every morning at seven o'clock, I pee like a baby," replies the old man.

"Good," says the doctor. "And how about your bowel movements?"

"Eight o'clock, every morning, I poop like clockwork," says the old guy.

"So what's the problem then?" asks the doctor.

"Well," replies the old man, "I don't get up until nine!"

old Lady at the Doctor's

An old woman goes to the doctor's office. The doctor gives her a checkup and says, "I need to do stool, blood and urine tests on you."

The woman says, "Well, can I just leave my underwear? Bingo starts in half an hour."

Nice Nurses

A family brings their elderly mother to a nursing home. The nurses give her a bath and then put her in a chair at a window to enjoy the view.

After a while, the old lady slowly starts to lean over sideways in her chair. Two nurses quickly run over to her and straighten up the old lady. Again, the woman starts to tilt to the other side. The nurses rush back again to put her upright. This goes on all morning.

Question:
Have you ever seen a bunny with his nose so runny?

Answer:
Well, don't think it's funny, because it's-not.

In the afternoon, the woman's family comes to visit and asks her, "Are the nurses treating you all right?"

"Yes, they're pretty nice," the old woman replies. "Except they won't let you fart!"

Punk!

A young punk gets on the bus. He has spiked, multi-colored hair that's green, purple and orange. He's wearing baggy jeans, a torn T-shirt and worn-out running shoes. His entire face and body are covered with piercings, and his earrings are long, bright feathers.

The punk sits down in the only empty seat that's directly across from an old man who glares at him for the next five miles.

Finally, the punk starts to feel self-conscious and shouts at the old man, "What are you looking at, you old fart! Didn't you ever do anything wild when you were young?"

The old man replies, "Yeah, back when I was young and in the army, I got really drunk one night in Hong Kong and married a parrot. I thought maybe you were my son."

Curious Cop

One day a young man is stuck in heavy traffic that isn't moving at all, and he really has to take a poop. So he gets out of his truck, goes over to a bush and takes a poop in his baseball cap. He can't leave his hat there because his name is on it. He takes his hat, and on the way to his truck, he sees a police officer. He covers the hat with his hand.

The police officer comes over and asks, "Hey, mister, what do you have in that hat?"

The guy says, "It's a bird, and it's hurt."

The police officer says, "Let me see the bird."

The man says, "Sorry, I can't. If I take my hand away, it will try to fly away."

The police officer says again, "Let me see the bird."

The man repeats himself, telling the cop that the bird might fly away.

The police officer is starting to get angry and says to the man. "Listen! Take your hand away, and I will reach in really fast and the bird won't fly away!"

The guy says, "Okay." And he slowly removes his hand.

The police officer quickly reaches in and grabs a handful of poop. "What is this?" the cop screams as he pulls his hand out.

The man replies, "You scared the crap out of the bird!"

Chapter THREE

Animals Are Gross, Too

If a park ranger farts in the forest, and there is no one to smell it, does it still smell?

A Bad Day

Two bats are hanging upside down in a cave.

One asks the other, "Do you remember your worst day last year?"

The other bat says, "Yes, I do. It was the day I had diarrhea!"

Monkey Butt

Sam walks into a pool hall with his pet monkey. He orders a Coke, and while he's drinking

Question:
What monster sits on the end of your finger?

Answer:
The boogie man.

it, the monkey runs around and jumps up on the pool table and grabs the cue ball. The monkey sticks the ball in its mouth and swallows it.

The owner of the pool hall is mad and says to the guy, "Did you see what your monkey just did?"

"No. What did my stupid monkey do?" says Sam.

"Well, he just swallowed the cue ball off the pool table!" says the owner.

"Yeah, well, I hope it makes him sick because he's been driving me crazy," says Sam, who then finishes his Coke and leaves.

Two weeks later, Sam returns to the pool hall with the monkey. He orders a Coke, and the monkey starts running wild around the room again. While Sam is drinking his Coke, the monkey finds some peanuts on the floor. The monkey grabs one of the peanuts and sticks it up his butt, then pulls it out and eats it.

The owner sees this and is disgusted. "Did you see what your monkey just did?" he asks Sam.

"What now?" says Sam, who is busy playing pool.

"Well, he stuck a peanut up his bum, then pulled it out and ate it!" says the owner.

ANIMALS ARE GROSS, TOO

"Well, what do you expect?" replies Sam. "Ever since he ate that cue ball, he measures everything first!"

A Smart Cowboy

A cowboy rides his horse up to a saloon.

All the customers stare at the cowboy when he kisses his horse on the butt before coming in and asking for a drink.

The bartender serves him a beer and says, "Do you mind if I ask you why you would kiss your horse on the butt?"

The cowboy says, "It's because I got chapped lips."

The bartender asks, "Does doing that help them heal?"

Question:
Why did the fish jump out of the water?

Answer:
Because the seaweed (the sea weed)!

Cowboy replies, "No, but it keeps me from licking my lips."

Nice Brother!

Mother: "Why did you put a frog in your sister's bed?"

Jimmy: "I couldn't find a snake."

What's gross?

A cat barfing all over the floor.

What's grosser than that?

Another cat eating it up.

Frog Love

A small frog goes to a fortuneteller and asks if he is going to meet a young girl in his future.

The psychic says, "Yes, you are."

The frog replies, "Really? Where? At a party?"

The psychic says, "In biology class."

Fly Love

Two male flies are buzzing around, looking for pretty female flies. One fly spots a real cutie sitting on a pile of cow poop and dives down towards her.

"Pardon me," he asks, turning on his best charm, "but is this stool taken?"

Vacuum Salesman

A vacuum cleaner salesman walks into a house, and without saying a word, he starts to empty a huge bag of horse poop onto the floor.

The little boy who answers the door screams in disgust and tells him not to do that.

The salesman looks at him and says, "Look, son, trust me. What this vacuum cleaner doesn't pick up, I'll eat!"

The boy looks at him with a smile and says, "Do you like your poop with sauce? The power isn't working!"

Rover in Heaven

One day, little Tommy takes his dog for a walk, and the dog runs away and gets hit by a car and dies. Tommy's mom and dad try to make Tommy feel better.

Question:
What did one burp say to the other?

Answer:
Let's be stinkers and come out the other end.

"You know, Tommy," says his dad, "it's not your fault that Rover died. It was just his time."

Tommy is still sad and goes up to his room, crying.

Tommy's dad goes upstairs, sits down on the bed next to Tommy and says, "Don't worry about your dog, Tommy. Rover is probably up in heaven with God, happy and enjoying himself, so you don't have to feel sad anymore."

Tommy turns to his father and says, "What the heck would God want with a dead dog?"

What's gross?

A dog digging in the kitty litter for nuggets.

Question:
What's long, green and hangs off trees?

Answer:
Giraffe snot.

What's grosser than that?

When the owner gives the dog heck, it tries to make nice with a big, sloppy kiss on the owner's face.

Animal Lover

A teenager in a supermarket goes up to the cashier and places two cans of dog food on the counter.

The cashier asks, "Do you have a dog, young man?"

"Yes, it's at home," replies the teenager.

"Well, to be able to sell you the dog food, I must see the dog. That is our store policy," says the cashier.
The teenager leaves the store without saying another word.

The next day, the teenager goes to the same store and places two cans of cat food on the counter.

"Do you own a cat?" asks the cashier.

"Yes, I do. It's at home," says the teenager.

"Well, I am sorry. I must see the cat before I can sell you cat food," says the cashier.

The next day the teenager returns to the store and walks directly to the same cashier. He has a brown paper bag in his hand. "Here," he says to the cashier, "put your hand in here."

The cashier puts her hand in the brown paper bag. "It is all soft and warm," she says.

"Yes, that's right," says the teenager. "I need to buy two rolls of toilet paper."

Chapter
FOUR

Crunchy, Chewy and Icky

There are no winners when a broccoli fart occurs.

Does This Taste Weird?

John: "I didn't use a recipe for the pizza we just ate. I made it from scratch off the top of my head!"

Bob: "Hmmm. I thought I tasted dandruff."

Mmmm, Strawberries

A little boy sees a man at the side of the road who has a truck load of cow poop. The boy asks him what he is going to do with it.

Question:
How can you tell which end of a worm is which?

Answer:
Tickle it in the middle and see which end smiles.

The man tells the little boy, "I'm taking it home to put on my strawberries."

The little boy looks up at the man and says, "I don't know where you come from, but where I come from, we put cream and sugar on our strawberries."

Eating Habits

A boy walks into a doctor's office. He has a cucumber up his nose, a carrot in his left ear and a banana in his right ear.

"I don't feel so good. What's the matter with me?" he asks the doctor.

The doctor replies, "You're not eating properly."

Soup

Two travelers in Africa are captured by a tribe of cannibals who put them in a very large pot of water, build a huge fire under it and leave them there.

A few minutes later, one of the travelers starts to laugh and can't stop.

The other traveler can't believe it! He says, "What's wrong with you? We're being boiled alive, and they're gonna eat us! What's so funny at a time like this?"

The other traveler replies, "I just peed in the soup!"

A Bumpy Airplane Ride

A little guy gets on a plane and sits next to the window.

Five minutes later, a big, heavy, mean-looking man sits down in the seat next to the little guy and immediately falls asleep.

The little guy starts to feel a little airsick, but he's afraid to wake the big guy up to ask if he can go to the bathroom. He knows he can't climb over him, and so the little guy just sits there, looking at the big guy and trying to decide what to do.

Suddenly, the plane hits an air pocket, and the little guy starts to feel really sick. He can't hold it in any longer, and he pukes all over the big man's chest.

A few minutes later, the big man wakes up, looks down and sees the vomit all over him.

Before the big man can say anything, the little guy says, "So, are you feeling better now?"

Menu from the Restaurant "You Kill It, We Grill It"

DINNER SPECIALS

Center-line Bovine......$5.99
(Tastes real good, straight from the hood.)

The Chicken that Didn't Cross the Road........$4.49
(What a dumb cluck.)

Flat Cat *(served as a single or in a stack)*

Single Flat Cat $1.99
Double Flat Cat $2.79
Flat Cat Stack... $4.99
Flat Cat Family Pack *(with kittens)*..................... $9.00

Chunk of Skunk $7.49
(Smells real good!)

Smidgen of Pigeon $3.49
(Tastes so good, you'll coo for more.)

Road Toad $2.99
(Jump into this dish, and you'll croak for more.)

Shake 'n' Bake Snake $3.00
(It's long and chewy, with 40 secret spices.)

Swirl of Squirrel $2.49
(You'll go nuts for our squirrel.)

Rigor Mortis Tortoise................................ $7.00
(Slowly aged to perfection.)

Smear of Deer $8.99
(You'll eat Bambi's heart out and love it!)

Special of the Day! $9.00
(Guess that mess! If you can guess it, you eat it for free!)

OUR DAILY TAKE-OUT LUNCH SPECIAL!

Bag 'n' Gag: Anything Dead, in Bread................ $2.49

Good Sons

Three sons leave home to make their fortunes, and they all become very rich. They get together one day to talk about what they each bought for their mother.

"Well," says the first son, "I bought Mom a huge house in Beverly Hills."

"I bought her a Mercedes and hired a full-time driver for her," says the second son.

"I've got you both beat," says the third son. "I bought her a parrot that can recite any Bible verse you tell it to."

A few days later, the mother sends a thank you letter to all of her three sons: "Gerald, the house you bought was too big. I only live in one room, but I have to clean the entire house. Mike, the car is useless because I don't go anywhere because I'm too old. But Robert, you knew exactly what I like. The chicken was delicious! Thank you!"

Fancy Restaurant

A young man walks into a fancy restaurant for dinner. The room is nicely decorated, with soft lighting and beautiful music playing in the background.

Question:
Did you hear about the cannibal who arrived late to the dinner party?

Answer:
The guests gave him the cold shoulder.

The waiter goes up to the man and asks, "What would you like to order?"

The man orders French onion soup, and the waiter quickly brings him the soup. It smells great and has a layer of golden cheese melted across the top. But the man notices that the waiter's thumb is sticking into the bowl, right into his soup! The man decides not to say anything and enjoys the soup, which is really good.

For the next course, the man orders steak, and again, the waiter's thumb is sticking into the warm gravy. For dessert, the man orders a warm plum pudding, and again the waiter's thumb is sticking in the pudding.

As the man is finishing the dessert, the waiter comes over and says, "How was your dinner, sir?"

The man looks up at him and says, "Well, the restaurant design is quite nice, the food was good, probably the best I've ever eaten, but the service... well..."

The waiter asks, "Was there something wrong with the service?"

The man replies, "Oh, you were very good all right, but when you brought the soup, I noticed your thumb was in it, and when you brought the steak, well, again, your thumb was in the gravy. And the same thing happened with the pudding—that big thumb again. This is such a nice place, how could you do such a thing?"

Question:
Why do elephants have flat feet?
Answer:
To stamp out burning ducks.

The waiter is embarrassed and replies, "Well, if you must know, my thumb is infected, and the doctor advised me to keep it as warm as possible."

The man explodes. "Infected thumb! That's awful! If you wanna keep it warm, you can shove it up your bum!"

The waiter says, "Oh, I do that in the kitchen, but in the dining room, it doesn't look very nice."

Tough Tomatoes!

A family of three tomatoes—a mom, dad and baby tomato—are walking downtown one day when the baby tomato starts to fall behind her mom and dad. The father tomato walks back to the baby tomato and stomps on her, squashing her into a red paste, and says, "Ketchup!"

Things Cannibals Say

"If you don't change the direction, you're going to end up at the wrong end."

"People who go out of their way to help others have great taste."

"An eye for an eye leaves everybody blind, but not hungry."

"Don't give up when the pace seems slow, you may succeed at another morgue."

"A journey of 100 trillion cells begins with a single nibble."

"The only difference between a big shot and a little shot is that the big shot takes longer to chew."

"You don't know what your appetite can get away with until you try. Or are tried."

"If you carry your childhood with you, you should probably go to the bathroom soon."

"Never try to keep up with the neighbors. Have them over for dinner instead."

Chapter FIVE

Kids Have Cooties

If you were a booger, I'd pick you first.

Know Your ABCs!

Billy is in grade two and asks his teacher if he can go to the bathroom.

The teacher says, "Yes, you can, but first say the alphabet."

Billy says,

"A B C D E F G H I J K L M N O Q R S T U V W X Y Z ."

The teacher says, "That's almost correct, Billy, but where is the 'P'?"

Billy says, "Running down my leg."

Shhhh!

A mother takes her little boy to church.

While in church, the little boy says, "Mommy, I have to pee!"

The mother says to the little boy, "It's not polite to say the word 'pee' in church. So, from now on, whenever you have to use the washroom, just tell me that you have to whisper."

The next Sunday, the little boy goes to church with his father, and during the service he says to him, "Daddy, I have to whisper."

The father looks at him and says, "Okay, just whisper in my ear."

Girl Cooties

Little Mikey: "Why do girls wear makeup and perfume?"

Little Johnny: "Because they're ugly and they stink."

Wooden Eye

A boy is involved in a terrible car accident and loses one of his eyes. The doctor replaces the eye with a fake wooden eye. Some months pass, and the boy's friends come to visit him. They are very worried because he has not been out of the house for months. They tell him that there is a party at another friend's house that night. The boy finally agrees to go.

When they get to the party, everyone is dancing and having a good time. The friends tell him that he should ask a girl to dance. The boy sees a girl sitting by herself. He decides to walk over to her and ask her to dance. As he gets closer, he notices that she has a harelip. He thinks to himself, "What a pair we would make! My wooden eye and her harelip." The boy walks up to the girl and asks if she would like to dance.

She replies, "Oh, would I, would I!"

He points at her and says, "Harelip, harelip!"

Fun at the Playground

A boy gets off a merry-go-round at the park and barfs all over himself. "Oh-oh," he says to his friend,

Question:
If you fall into an outhouse toilet, how long will you be in there?

Answer:
It depends on how many moons you see.

"I puked on my shirt. If my mom finds out, she's gonna kill me."

"No problem," says his rich friend, as he sticks 10 dollars in the boy's shirt pocket. "Just tell her some kid puked on you and he gave you some money to pay the cleaning bill."

So the boy goes home and tells his mom the story. She reaches into his pocket and finds not one but two $10 bills. "Why is there so much money?" she asks.

"Oh, yeah, he pooped in my pants, too."

Clean Dog

A boy walks into a store and buys 10 boxes of sandwich baggies. The store clerk is curious and asks the boy, "What do you do with all of those baggies?"

The boy replies, "I taught my dog to swallow them, and now he can poop in little plastic bags!"

How Stinky Are You?

You are so stinky you make Right Guard turn left, Secret tell it all and Speed Stick slow down.

You smell so bad that when you walk by, the skunks get high.

Your breath is so bad that your teeth are making plans to escape.

Your breath is so bad that your toothbrush prays every night.

Your breath smells so bad that you have to get prescription strength Tic-Tacs.

You smell so bad that when you walk down the street, the homeless offer you soap.

You smell so bad that the only dis I want to give you is a disinfectant.

You smell so bad that when you walk by the bathroom door, the toilet flushes itself.

Teamwork

After traveling for four hours, a family in a minivan pulls into the only remaining campsite on a busy long weekend. Four children jump from the van and quickly start to unload the camping gear and set up the tent. The two boys rush to gather firewood, while the two girls help their mother set up the camp stove and cooking utensils.

Question:
What do you give an elephant with diarrhea?

Answer:
Lots of room.

A camper in the next campsite is surprised to see all the kids work so fast. He says to their father, "Wow, sir, that is a great display of teamwork!"

The father replies, "Thank you. I have a system. No one gets to go to the bathroom until the camp is set up."

Cooties All over

A pretty teenager goes up to the counter at McDonalds. She smiles at the boy behind the counter and tells him to come closer. When he does, she begins to gently touch his cheek, which is slowly turning bright red. "Are you the owner?" she asks while she softly strokes his face with both hands.

"No," he replies. "I'm just the manager."

"Can you get him for me? I need to speak to him," she asks, running her hands up to his ears and then into his hair.

"I'm afraid I can't," says the manager, his face turning redder with all her attention. "He's in the back room doing some work right now. Is there anything I can do?"

"Yes, there is. I need you to give him a message," she says, popping two of her fingers into his

Question:
What do you get when you eat a prune pizza?

Answer:
Pizzeria.

mouth and allowing him to suck on them gently.

"Tell him," she says, "that there is no toilet paper or hand soap in the ladies washroom."

Question:
What did the dad say when his son said, "Dad, I'm tired of walking in circles"?

Answer:
"Be quiet, or I'll nail your other foot to the ground."

Girls Fart Too

A young teenager is sitting alone in a restaurant one night. She is waiting for her date and wants to make sure everything is perfect. So, as she bends down in her chair to get the mirror from her purse, she accidentally farts loudly just as the waiter walks up to her table.

Sitting up straight, her face red from embarrassment because she knows everyone in the place heard her, she turns to the waiter and shouts, "Stop that!"

The waiter looks at and says, "Sure, Miss, which way was it headed?"

A Ribbon Story

Once upon a time, there were two friends, a girl and a boy. The girl had a thick ribbon tied around her neck, and every day the boy asked her why she wore the ribbon, but she would never tell him.

The girl and boy grew up together and fell in love, and still, she would not tell him why she had the ribbon tied around her neck. They got married, had a family and grew old together, and still, she would not tell him why she wore the ribbon around her neck.

Then the day finally came when she said to him, "I'll show why I keep this ribbon around my neck." Slowly she unraveled the ribbon, and her head fell off.

The end.

Rude Clerk

A young woman is shopping at a grocery store. She picks up a quart of skim milk, two loaves of whole wheat bread, one dozen eggs and some carrots. She goes to the checkout line.

"You must be single," the clerk says to her.

Amazed at how smart the clerk is, the woman says, "Yes, I am. But how could you tell?"

"Because you're ugly."

What's That?

A girl walks up to a boy in the school cafeteria and sits down next to him. The girl notices that the boy is studying something closely between his fingers.

"What do you have there?" asks the girl.

"I don't know," replies the boy. "But it looks like plastic and feels like rubber!"

"Hmm, let me take a look!" the girl says, grabbing it and rolling it between her fingers.

"Yeah, you're right," says the girl. "It does look like plastic but feels like rubber. Where did you get it from?"

The boy replies, "Out of my nose!"

Gone Fishing!

Little Jake and Bob are sitting out on a lake ice-fishing. Bob is having no luck at all catching a fish, but Jake has been pulling fish after fish out of his hole in the ice. Bob keeps on trying to catch a fish but still has no luck. After an hour, Bob finally leans over and asks Jake what his secret is.

"Hmf mmm mm mmm mmm mmms mmm," says Jake.

"What did you say?" Bob asks, not understanding his friend.

"Hmf mmm mm mmm mmm mmmms mmm," Jake says again.

"I'm sorry, I still don't understand you," Bob says.

Jake spits something into his hand and says, "You've got to keep your worms warm."

Quick Runner

One day, a guy walks out of a store to see a kid peeing on his Ferrari.

"Hey!" says the man. "Why are you peeing on my car?"

"Because I feel like it!" says the rude kid.

"Tell you what," says the man. "I won't report you to the police if you can keep up with my Ferrari."

"Whatever," says the kid.

So the guy quickly gets in his car and drives off, going faster and faster, until he hits 100 miles per hour. Amazingly, the kid keeps up with him.

"I'm amazed!" says the man when he finally stops his Ferrari. "How did you keep with me?"

"It's easy," says the kid, out of breath, "when your hand is stuck in the door!"

Natural Hair

A teenager is admiring the hair of three girls. He walks up to one girl and says to her, "How'd you get such lovely blonde hair?"

Question:
What happens if you eat yeast and shoe polish?

Answer:
Every morning you'll rise and shine.

Taking her hand and gently running it through her hair, the girl answers, "It's natural."

The guy says to the second girl, "How'd you get such pretty brown hair?"

Fluffing her hair, the second girl says, "It's natural."

Finally the guy goes up to the third girl and asks, "How'd you get such cool green hair?"

Taking her hand and rubbing it up past her nose, then skimming it through the hair, she says, "It's natural."

Question:
What happened to the poor girl who swallowed the thermometer?

Answer:
She's dying by degrees.

Smoke Rings?

Three little boys are sitting around talking about their fathers.

The first boy says, "My dad can blow smoke rings."

The second boy says, "My dad can blow smoke rings out of his nose."

The third boy says, "Well, my dad can blow smoke rings out of his butt."

The first and second boys are amazed.

The second boy says, "Have you seen him do it?"

"No," says the third boy, "but I've seen the tobacco stains on his underwear."

Little Johnny in Church

Little Johnny is in church with his mom on Sunday when he suddenly feels like throwing up.

"Mom! I think I'm going to throw up!"

Johnny's mom says, "Oh, dear! I want you to run outside as fast as you can. Run across the lawn and go behind the

bushes. You can throw up behind the bushes and nobody will see you."

So Little Johnny runs out of the church. Less than a minute later, he returns to his seat next to his mom. He has the look of obvious relief on his young face.

"Did you make it all the way to the bushes, Johnny?" asks his mom.

"I didn't have to go that far, Mom. Just as I got to the front door, I found a box that had a sign on it saying, 'For the Sick.'"

A City Boy and a Country Boy

One day, two boys are walking through the forest when they see some rabbit turds. One of the boys, who is from Toronto, says, "What is that?"

"They're smart pills," says the other boy, who lives on a farm in Quebec. "If you eat them, they'll make you smarter."

So the boy from Toronto picks up the small, brown pieces and eats them. "These taste like crap!" he screams.

"See!" says the other boy. "You're getting smarter already."

Chapter SIX

That's Just Nasty!

Why fart and waste, when you can burp and taste?

Toilet Paper, Please

A young boy goes to the store to buy some toilet paper. The clerk at the store asks him what color he'd like. The boy replies, "White, and I'll color it myself."

Super-fun Happy Slide

Three boys are walking through the jungle when they come across a giant pot with a slide. A wizard is standing next to the pot, and he tells the boys to yell out whatever drink they want when they go down the slide, and that drink will appear when they hit the pot!

The first boy goes down the slide and screams, "Root beer!"

The second boy goes down the slide and yells, "Lemonade!"

The third little boy goes down the slide and yells, "Weeeeeeee!"

Yummy Peanuts!

An old man and a teenager work in the same office together. The teenager notices that the old man always seems to have a big jar of peanuts on his desk. The teenager loves peanuts!

Question:
What do spiders like to order at a fast food restaurant?

Answer:
Burgers and flies.

One day while the old man is away from his desk, the teenager can't resist them any longer so he walks over to the old man's desk, reaches into the jar and eats half the peanuts.

When the old man returns to his desk, the teenager feels guilty and tells the old man that he has eaten most of his peanuts.

The old man replies, "That's okay. Don't worry about it. Since I lost my teeth a few years ago, all I can do is lick the chocolate off the Glosettes."

Hungry Dog

Guest at a home: "Why does your dog sit there and watch me eat?"

Hostess: "I can't imagine... unless it's because you're using the plate he usually eats from."

Question:
What's the last thing that goes through a bug's mind when it hits a windshield?

Answer:
His butt!

oMG!

Two blonde girls from Ireland are walking around New York City. Before they left on their trip, they heard that Americans eat something called "dogs," so they both agree to try it when they arrive. As they're walking through the streets of New York, they hear someone yell, "Hot dogs! Get your hot dogs!" They rush over to the man to buy one for themselves. As the first blonde opens hers, her face turns white and she gasps, "What part did you get?!"

Definitely!

A teacher is explaining to her students the meaning of the word "definitely." She thinks that if each student uses the word in a sentence, they will understand it better. So one student gets up and says, "The sky is definitely blue."

The teacher says, "That's not true because clouds can make the sky look gray."

Another student says, "Grass is definitely green."

The teacher says, "Well, the grass can look yellow if you don't water it."

Then Little Johnny says, "Are there lumps in farts?"

The teacher replies, "Excuse me?!"

Little Johnny repeats, "Are there lumps in farts?"

The teacher says, "That isn't even a response to my question! But, no, there are no lumps in farts."

The student replies, "Then I definitely just pooped my pants!"

A Good Lesson!

A group of students who want to become doctors is gathered around an operating table for their first lesson with a dead body.

"If you want to be a doctor, you have to learn two special skills," the professor says to the students. "The first skill is courage. You can't be disgusted by anything involving the human body."

The professor then rolls the body over, sticks his finger into the corpse's bum, takes his finger out and then puts his finger in his mouth.

Question:
Why did Mickey Mouse get shot?

Answer:
Because Donald Ducked.

"Now it's your turn," he says to the students.

The students are horrified, but they all take turns dipping a finger into the butt and then suck on their fingers.

After everyone has finished, the professor says to them, "The second skill you must learn is observation. I stuck in my middle finger, and then I sucked on my index finger. Pay attention next time!"

How to be a Good Salesperson

The students in a grade five class return to school Monday morning very excited. Their weekend assignment was to sell something, then give a talk to the class about how to be a good salesperson.

Little Sally is first. "I sold Girl Guide cookies, and I made $30," she says proudly. "I told my customers that they would help a very good cause if they bought my cookies, and that's why I was successful."

"Very good," says the teacher.

Little Jenny is next. "I sold magazines," she says. "I made $45, and I explained to everyone that magazines would keep them up on current events."

"Very good, Jenny," says the teacher.

Question:
What is Mozart doing right now?

Answer:
Decomposing.

Eventually, it is Little Johnny's turn.

Little Johnny walks to the front of the classroom and dumps a box full of cash on the teacher's desk.

"I made $2000," he says.

"What?!" says the teacher. "What in the world were you selling?"

"Toothbrushes," says Little Johnny.

"Toothbrushes?" says the teacher. "How could you sell enough toothbrushes to make that much money?"

"Well, I found the busiest corner in town," says Little Johnny, "and I set up a 'Chip and Dip' stand, and I gave everybody who walked by a free sample. They all said the same thing: 'Hey, this tastes like crap!' Then I would say, 'It *is* crap. Wanna buy a toothbrush?'"

The Poopie List

Ghost Poopie: The kind where you feel the poopie come out, but there's no poopie in the toilet.

Clean Poopie: The kind where you poopie it out and see it in the toilet, but there is nothing on the toilet paper.

Wet Poopie: The kind where you wipe your butt 50 times, but it still feels unwiped, so you have to put some toilet paper between your butt cheeks so you don't ruin your underwear with a stain.

Second Wave Poopie: The kind that happens when you're done poopie-ing, and you've pulled your pants up to your knees when you realize you have to poopie some more.

Turtle Poopie: The kind of poopie that pops out a little and goes back in a few times before it finally comes out.

Pop-a-Vein-in-Your-Forehead Poopie: The kind where you strain so much to get it out that your eyes almost pop out of your head.

Lincoln Log Poopie: The kind of poopie that is so huge that you're afraid to flush without first breaking it into little pieces with the plunger.

Gassy Poopie: The kind where it's so noisy that everyone in the next room starts to giggle.

Drinker Poopie: The kind of poopie you have the morning after drinking too much sweet juice. You'll notice a lot of skid marks on the bottom of the toilet.

Corn Poopie: I think you know what this is!

Gee-I-Wish-I-Could-Poop Poopie: The kind where you want to poopie, but all you do is sit on the toilet and fart a few times.

Spinal Tap Poopie: That's the kind when it hurts so badly coming out that you swear the poopie was coming out of you sideways.

Wet Cheeks Poopie (also known as The Power Dump): The kind that comes out of your butt so fast that your bum cheeks get splashed with water.

Liquid Poopie: The kind where yellowish-brown liquid shoots you of your bum and splashes all over the toilet bowl.

Powerful Poopie: The kind that smells so bad your nose burns.

Dangling Poopie: This poopie refuses to drop into the toilet even though you know you are done poopie-ing. You just pray that shaking your butt a few times will cut it loose.

Question:
Why can't Jesus eat M&Ms?

Answer:
They keep falling through the holes in his hands.

The Rich Poopie: The kind of poopie that doesn't smell.

Surprise Poopie: This happens when you are not even on the toilet—because you are sure you only need to fart. But, oopsy! Yup, a poopie! Surprise!

Spot!

A teenager is invited to dinner at the home of his girlfriend and is meeting her parents for the first time. He is very nervous about meeting them, so by the time he arrives at their doorstep, his stomach is giving him a lot of problems. He has to fart, but he holds it in, but halfway through dinner, the teenager realizes he can't hold it in one second longer without exploding. So he lets out a tiny fart.

"Spot!" says his girlfriend's dad to the family dog that is lying next to the teenager.

Glad that the dad is blaming the dog, the teenager lets out another, slightly louder, fart.

"Spot!" the dad yells out again.

"I've got it made," the teenager thinks to himself. "One more, and I'll feel just fine." So he lets loose a really big one this time.

"Spot!" screams the dad. "Get over here before he poops on you!"

A Fart Poem

A belch is just one gust of wind,
That cometh from thy heart,
But if it takes the downward trend,
It turns into a fart.

Hungry?

A man walks into a restaurant, and he's feeling kind of low. He sits down at a table next to a man with leprosy, who also has his share of bad luck.

Question:
What is green and red and goes 100 miles per hour?

Answer:
A frog in a blender.

The man says to the waiter, "Gimme a strong coffee." When the waiter brings him the coffee, the man drinks it fast and then suddenly throws up.

The guy with leprosy says, "If I make you that sick, well, I will leave, okay?"

The other man says, "No, you ain't making me sick—it's the guy behind you. He's dipping his nachos into your back!"

Camping Blonde

Question:
What do you call a guy with no arms and no legs in a boiling pot?
Answer:
Stu.

One weekend, a blonde, a brunette and a redhead go camping. When they reach their campsite, the blonde woman suddenly has to go to the bathroom. She runs into the woods with her toilet paper.

The brunette and the redhead decide to play a joke on her. They skin a rabbit and sneak up on the blonde. They quietly place the rabbit guts behind the blonde and then run back to the campsite. Three minutes later, they hear a scream.

The brunette and the redhead wait for half an hour, and the blonde finally returns to the campsite, sweating. She says, "I had to poop so hard that I pooped my guts out. But thanks to God and these two fingers, I stuffed them back in."

Out for a Walk

Two young men are walking down the street towards each other. They are both dragging their right foot as they walk.

As they meet, one man looks at the other, points to his own right foot and says, "Snowboard accident, 2012."

The other points his thumb behind him and says, "Dog poop, 20 feet back."

Got Any Toilet Paper?

Two kids are walking through the forest when one says to the other that he has to go to the bathroom. "Well, go in the bushes," says his friend.

"What should I use to wipe my butt?"

"Use a five-dollar bill."

A few minutes later, the boy steps out of the bushes with poop all over his hands.

"What happened?" asks his friend.

"I didn't have five dollars, so I used quarters."

Robbery

Two young robbers break into a bank, but when they open the safe, there's no money, only boxes. One of the robbers opens a box and finds cups full of yogurt.

"We didn't find any money, but at least we have something to eat," he tells his partner. They eat as much as they can and then run out of the bank.

The next morning's newspaper reads: "Booger Research Lab Robbed."

Weird and Wild

**When someone yawns, do deaf people think
they're screaming?**

Taste Tester: True Story

Edwin Rose has one of the world's weirdest jobs. He is
a pet food taster for Safeway
stores in Canada.

A newspaper story said that
20-year-old Edwin spends
his working days
trying out different
canned foods made
for dogs and cats.
His job is to figure
out what kinds of
meat, sauces and
spices dogs and cats
will like to eat. All the
big pet food makers test

their dog and cat food by using animals, but Edwin, whose girlfriend calls him "Dog Breath," is the only human in the world known to have a job like this—and he likes it.

"I try to figure out from a dog or cat's perspective what they like or don't like about a particular pet food," he says. "Though I must confess that the premium cat foods are my favorite."

Just Wait and See

A small boy swallows some coins and is taken to a hospital. When his grandmother telephones the hospital to ask how he is doing, the nurse says, "No change yet."

Tap, Tap

A passenger sitting in the backseat of a taxi taps the driver on the shoulder to ask him a question. The driver screams, loses control of the car, nearly hits a bus, goes up on the sidewalk and stops just inches from a store window. For a second, everything goes quiet in the taxi, then the driver says, "Look, mister, don't ever do that again. You scared the daylights out of me!"

The passenger apologizes and says, "I didn't realize that a little tap on the shoulder would scare you so much."

The driver replies, "Sorry, it's not really your fault. Today is my first day as a taxi driver. I've been driving a funeral van for the last 25 years."

Pee, Please!

On the first day of school, the kindergarten teacher says to her class, "If anyone has to go to the bathroom, hold up two fingers." A little voice from the back of the room says, "How will that help?"

A New Baby!

Question:
What is grosser than gross?

Answer:
Having a dream about chocolate pudding and then waking up with a spoon in your bum.

For weeks, a six-year-old boy keeps telling his first-grade teacher about the baby brother or sister that is expected at his house. One day the boy's mother allows him to feel the movements of the unborn baby. The boy is very impressed, but he doesn't say anything. And he also stops telling his teacher about the new baby brother or sister. The teacher notices and asks the boy, "Tommy, whatever became of that baby brother or sister you were expecting at home?"

Tommy bursts into tears and says, "I think Mommy ate it!"

Question:
How do you kill the circus?

Answer:
You go for the juggler.

In the Jungle

A science teacher, a school janitor and a principal get lost in the Amazon on a school trip. They get captured by some huge Amazons who plan to torture them for trespassing on their land. The head of the tribe says to the teacher, "What do you want on your back for your whipping?"

The teacher replies, "I will take oil," thinking the whip will just slide off his back. They put oil on his back and whip him 10 times. When the whipping is over, the teacher has huge red welts on his back, and he can hardly move.

The Amazons haul the teacher away, and then say to the janitor, "What do you want on your back?"

"I will take nothing!" says the tough janitor. He stands there straight and takes his 10 lashings without a single moan.

"What will you take on your back?" the Amazons then ask the principal.

"I'll take the janitor."

Question:
How do you make a one-armed man fall out of a tree?

Answer:
Wave at him.

Accident

A little girl steps on a land mine and is taken to the hospital for surgery.

When she wakes up, she says to the doctor, "Something is wrong...I can't feel my legs!"

The doctor says, "Yes, I know. We had to amputate both your arms."

Pirate Life

A young boy is walking along the docks one day admiring the big ships, when a man walks up behind him and says, "Are you thinking of becoming a sailor?"

"Yes, I am!" replies the boy.

"Well," the man says, "I have sailed for many years, and I had many adventures."

The boy looks the man up and down and sees that he has an eye patch, a peg leg and a hook.

"I'd love to hear about your adventures," says the boy.

"Okay," the man says. "One time, a long time ago, I was sailing around the world when I came across some pirates. They boarded my boat and wanted to rob me, but I fought them all until there was only one pirate left. But before he escaped, he cut off my leg!"

Question:
What do you call a vegetarian with diarrhea?

Answer:
A salad shooter.

"That sounds terrible!" exclaims the boy.

"Aye, lad, it was, but I got over it, and I continued sailing the seas."

"How did you get the hook?" asks the boy.

"Well, I was once again sailing around the world, and on my way home I met the same pirate, and he had a whole new crew. They boarded my boat again, and I fought them all, down to the last man. Only this time, before he got away, he cut off my hand!"

"That's awful!" the boy once again exclaims.

"Aye, lad, but again I got over it, and I continued sailing the seas."

"Tell me how you got the eye patch! Was it the pirates again?" asks the boy.

"No, lad. This time I was just out fishing one day when I heard the cry of a seagull, and when I looked up, it crapped in my eye!"

"Pardon me, sir, but I didn't know you could lose an eye from gull poop?" says the boy.

"Well, my boy, it was the first day with my new hook!"

Question:
What do you call a man with no arms and no legs in a lake?
Answer:
Bob.

Your Turn!

In a city park, there are two statues, one female and the other male. These two statues have faced each other for many years.

Early one morning, an angel appears before the statues and says, "Since the two of you have been good statues and have brought enjoyment to many people in this park, I'm giving you the gift of life. You have 30 minutes to do whatever you desire." And with that command, the statues come to life.

The two statues smile at each other, run toward some nearby woods and dive behind a couple of bushes. The angel smiles to himself as he listens to the two statues giggling and the bushes rustling.

After 15 minutes, the two statues come out from the bushes, smiling. Puzzled, the angel looks at his watch and says to the two statues, "You still have 15 minutes. Would you like to continue?"

The male statue looks at the female statue and says, "Do you want to do it again?"

Smiling, the female statue says, "Sure. But this time *you* hold the pigeon down, and *I'll* poop on its head!"

Cannibal Restaurant

Three young men get lost in the desert and wander around for days with no food and little water.

One day, just as they are finally about to give up, they come across a sign that says "Cannibal's Restaurant."

Next to the door is a large menu board. With the little energy they have left, the three men slowly stand up and read the menu:

"Fried Principal $12.00
BBQ Math Teacher $14.00
Steamed Old Janitor $198.50"

The men go inside the restaurant, and a waiter comes to take their order. Before they order, one of the men asks the waiter, "Can you help me understand your menu, please? The first two items are priced about the same, but the third item, the janitor, is priced so much higher. Why is that?"

"Are you kidding?" replies the waiter. "Do you know how hard it is to *clean* one of those old guys?"

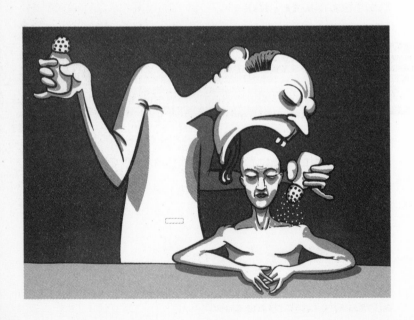

Poop Poem

I heard some strange talk from my turds;

"Pfft, plop, ker-plunk" were their words.

I turned to talk, then,

To my new little friends,

But they drowned silent, unheard.

I Remember When

Two vomits are walking down the street when one of them starts to cry.

"What's wrong with you?" asks the first vomit.

"Ohhhh," says the second vomit, "this is the area I was brought up in!"

Gross!

What's grosser than gross?

Siamese twins joined at the mouth, and one of them throwing up.

Question:
What has two arms and sucks?

Answer:
Justin Bieber.

Did You Hear This one?

"I see," said the blind man, peeing into the wind. "It's all coming back to me now."

Chapter
EIGHT

Jokes Not to Tell Parents

Laugh and the world laughs with you. Fart, and they'll stop laughing.

Pine fresh!

An Avon Lady is delivering makeup in a high-rise building and is riding in the elevator to the 10th floor. Suddenly, she has the powerful urge to fart. Since no one is in the elevator, she lets it go—and it's a doozy.

Of course, the elevator then stops at the next

floor, so she quickly uses some Avon Pine-Scented Spray to cover up the smell. A boy enters the elevator and immediately makes a face.

Question:
How do you make a Kleenex dance?

Answer:
You put a little boogie in it.

"Holy cow! What's that smell?" he says.

"I don't know," says the lady. "I don't smell anything. What does it smell like to you?"

"Like someone pooped a Christmas tree."

Can You Hear Me Now?

Two young men sneak into the yard of a blind man to see if they can steal something of value. The blind man hears them and opens his door with a shotgun in his hands.

The two young men, noticing that the man is blind, stand very still.

The blind man calls out, "Marco!" There is silence. He calls out again, "Marco!" More silence. He screams out one more time, "Marco!"

One of the young men, tired of the silly game, yells out, "Ha! We aren't going to fall for that—"

Bang!

Where's Your Manners!

Two flies are sitting on a pile of poop. One fly lets out a fart. The other fly looks at him and says, "Hey, do you mind? I'm trying to eat here!"

Hunting oops

Two new hunters are out in the woods, when one of them falls to the ground. He doesn't seem to be breathing, and his eyes roll back in his head. The other hunter takes out his cellphone and calls 911. He gasps to the operator, "My friend is dead! What should I do?"

The operator, in a calm soothing voice says, "Just take it easy. I can help. First, let's make sure he's dead."

There is a silence, and then a shot is heard.

The guy's voice comes back on the line. He says, "Okay, now what?"

Bad Grandma!

Little Tony is staying with his grandmother for a few days. After playing outside with the other kids for a while, he goes into the house and says, "Grandma, what

Question:
What's brown and sits in the forest?

Answer:
Winnie's Pooh.

is it called when two people are sleeping in the same room, and one is on top of the other?"

The grandmother is a little surprised by his question, but decides to tell him the truth. "It's called sexual intercourse, my dear."

Little Tony says, "Oh, okay," and he goes back outside to the other kids.

A few minutes later, Tony goes back into the house and says angrily, "Grandma, it's not called 'sexual intercourse'! It's called 'bunk beds'! And Jimmy's mom wants to talk to you right now."

Is My Girlfriend okay?

Harry answers the telephone, and it's a doctor calling from a hospital.

The doctor says, "Your girlfriend was in a serious car accident, and I have bad news and good news. The bad news is she has lost all use of both arms and both legs, and she will need help eating and going to the bathroom for the rest of her life."

Harry says, "My God. That's awful! What's the good news?"

The doctor says, "I'm just kidding. She's dead."

Right on!

Did you hear about the guy who lost his left arm and his left leg?

Well, he's all right now.

A Helping Hand

A police officer is driving past a restaurant and notices two bikes parked in the middle of the road. He stops and sees two boys, one with his finger up the butt of the other boy.

"Hey, what's going on here?" the police officer asks.

The boy replies, "My friend doesn't feel well, and I'm trying to make him vomit so he'll feel better."

The cop says, "Umm, I think you should be sticking your finger down his throat."

The boy replies, "That's what I'm going to do next!"

Chili Anyone?

A man goes into a cafe and sits down at the counter. A waitress comes to take his order, and he asks her, "What's the special of the day?"

Question:
What do girls call farts?

Answer:
Butt whispers.

"Chili," she says, "but the gentleman next to you got the last bowl."

The man says he'll just have coffee, and the waitress goes to get it. As he waits for his coffee, he notices the man next to him hasn't eaten his chili.

"Are you going to eat your chili?" he asks.

"No, help yourself," says the man.

The man picks up a spoon and begins to eat the chili. When he gets halfway through the bowl, he sees a dead mouse in the bottom of the bowl. He suddenly doesn't feel well, and he pukes the chili he had just eaten back into the bowl.

The man says to him, "Yeah, that's as far as I got, too."

Dear God

A kid has been praying every night for a new bike. After doing this for weeks and not getting the bike, he realizes the Lord doesn't work that way, so he steals a bike and then asks God to forgive him.

Question:
What do you call a garbage bag full of mutilated laboratory monkeys?

Answer:
Rhesus Pieces.

Too Disgusting to Read!

Two starving homeless men are walking through an alley when one of them sees a dead cat. He hasn't eaten for days so he runs over, sits down and starts to eat the cat, tearing the meat from its limbs.

He says to the other guy, "Hey, I know you're hungry, too. Why don't you eat some of this cat?"

"Oh no!" replies the second man. "That cat has been dead for days. He's all stiff and cold and smelly!"

The first man says, "Okay, suit yourself," and continues to eat everything—skin, muscle, guts, all but the skeleton.

A few hours later, as the two men are walking down the street, the first guy says, "Oh, I don't feel so good. I think there might have been something wrong with that cat." And just then, he pukes up a huge puddle of rotten cat flesh and guts with stomach bile mixed in, all half digested and looking like mush.

The second homeless man sits down next to the puddle and says, "Now you're talkin'! It's been months since I had a warm meal!"

Hungry Cannibals

Question:
What do you call a guy with no arms and no legs hanging on the wall?
Answer:
Art.

Two cannibals come across a dead body in the forest. One says to the other, "I'll start at the head, you start at the feet."

They start to eat, and after a while, the cannibal at the head yells to the other one, "Hey, how's it going?"

The other replies, "I'm having a ball!"

Getting mad, the cannibal at the head yells, "Hey, slow down! You're eating too fast!"

Can I Give You a Hand?

A man working with an electric saw accidentally saws off all 10 fingers. He rushes to the hospital. The doctor says, "Quick, give me the fingers, and I'll see what I can do."

Question:
What do you get when a dinosaur blows its nose?

Answer:
Out of the way!

"But I don't have the fingers!"

"What? Why didn't you bring the fingers with you?" asks the surprised doctor.

"Doc, I couldn't pick them up."

Cross-eyed Cow

One day, a farmer is checking his cows when he notices that one of them is completely cross-eyed. He takes the cow to the vet. The vet takes one look at the cow, sticks a tube up the cow's butt and blows into the tube until the cow's eyes straighten out.

The vet charges the farmer $100, and the farmer goes home happy. About a week later, the cow's eyes are cross-eyed again, but this time the farmer figures he can probably take care of it himself instead of paying the vet $100.

The farmer calls his hired hand over, and together they put a tube up the cow's butt. The farmer puts his lips to the tube and starts to blow. Strangely, nothing happens—the cow's eyes are still cross-eyed—so he asks his young hired hand to give it a try.

The hired hand removes the tube, turns it around, puts it in the cow's butt and starts to blow.

"Are you crazy!" says the farmer, horrified. "What are you doing?"

"Well, I wasn't gonna use the same side that *you* put your lips on."

A Smelly Bottom

The blonde walks into a drugstore and asks the pharmacist for some bottom deodorant. The pharmacist explains to her that they don't sell anything called "bottom deodorant," and never have. The blonde tells him that she has bought the stuff from this store all the time, and she wants some more.

"I'm sorry," says the pharmacist, "we don't have any."

"But I always get it here!" says the blonde.

"Do you have the box it comes in?"

"Yes!" says the blonde, "I'll go and get it."

She returns with the container and hands it to the pharmacist. He looks at it and says to her, "This is just a normal stick of underarm deodorant."

The angry blonde grabs the container back and reads out loud from the container: "To apply, push up bottom."

Question:
What do you call someone who doesn't fart in public?

Answer:
A private tooter.

Bingo!

Question:
What's invisible and smells like carrots?

Answer:
Rabbit farts.

Mike goes to his church bingo club every Sunday, where a funny door prize is given out. One week, Mike wins a toilet brush.

"What is this?" he asks the bingo caller.

"Why, it's a toilet brush," says the bingo caller, smiling,

"Oh, I see," says Mike. A couple weeks later, the bingo caller sees Mike and asks him how the brush is working.

"Well, it's okay, but I think I'll go back to using toilet paper."

At the Swimming Pool

A little boy is at an outdoor swimming pool.

The lifeguard blows his whistle at the boy and yells, "Hey, kid! Don't pee in the pool!"

The boy replies, "But everybody does it!"

"Not from the diving board!" shouts the lifeguard.

Chapter
NINE

More Funny Riddles

Question:
How do you wake up Lady Gaga?

Answer:
Poke'r Face.

Question:
Why are frogs so happy?

Answer:
They eat whatever bugs them!

Question:
What's grosser than gross?

Answer:
Eating a bowl of corn flakes only to discover that it's really your little brother's scab collection.

Question:
Why do giraffes have long necks?

Answer:
Because they have smelly feet.

Question:
Why do gorillas have big nostrils?

Answer:
Because they have big fingers to pick it.

Question:
Why don't elephants like to eat clowns?

Answer:
Because they taste funny.

Question:
What's worse than finding a worm in your apple?

Answer:
Finding half a worm.

Question:
What did the cannibal do after he dumped his girlfriend?

Answer:
He wiped his bum.

Question:

How do you find Ronald McDonald at a nude beach?

Answer:

You look for the sesame seed buns.

Question:

What do you call a girl with no arms and no legs hammered into a piece of wood?

Answer:

Peg.

Question:

What do you get when you mix beans and onions?

Answer:

Tear gas.

Question:

How do you get holy water?

Answer:

Boil the hell out of it.

Question:

Why don't they have any toilet paper in KFC?

Answer:

Because it's finger-licking good!

Question:

How can you tell if a girl is wearing pantyhose?

Answer:

Her ankles swell up when she farts.

Question:
Why did Tigger stick his head down the toilet?

Answer:
He was looking for Pooh.

Question:
What did one cannibal say to the other while they were eating a clown?

Answer:
"Do you taste something funny?"

Question:
Did you hear about the giant with diarrhea?

Answer:
You didn't? It's all over town!

Question:
I have a green nose, three red lips and four purple ears. What am I?

Answer:
Ugly!

Question:
Why did the skeleton burp?

Answer:
Because it didn't have the guts to fart.

ABOUT THE AUTHOR

JAMES ALLAN EINSTEIN has been collecting kids jokes of all kinds since...well...since he was a kid! In fact, he still thinks of himself as a great big kid because he still gets a kick out of grossing people out with vomit and bathroom jokes, and he also loves the quintessential knock-knock joke! Invariably, his friends will groan when he says excitedly, "I've got a new one for you!"

ABOUT THE ILLUSTRATOR

ROGER GARCIA EINSTEIN is a self-taught freelance illustrator who works in acrylics, ink and digital media. His illustrations have been published in humor books, children's books, newspapers and educational material.

When Roger is not at home drawing, he gives cartooning workshops at various elementary schools, camps and local art events. Roger also enjoys participating with colleagues in art shows and painting murals in schools and public places.